Chords of Faith, Notes of Grace

Life, Music, and Ministry

Billye Bowman

ISBN: 978-1-942923-86-2 (paperback)

Our Written Lives | San Antonio, Texas
www.OurWrittenLives.com

Fonts licensed for commercial use.

Dedication

This book is dedicated to my children, Vance, Grant, and Bethany, and their spouses, Dana, Kellie, and Chad. They have all lived many of these adventures with me. The road has not been easy, but you are overcomers! You make me proud every day!

To my grandchildren, Kaylie, Zac, Kendall, Zathan, Brooklyn, Miranda, Evan, Colin, and Mason, and their spouses, Frankie, Hannah, and Bri. "Seek ye first the kingdom of God . . . " I hope this book is a blessing to you. All of you are special to me.

To my great-granddaughters, Ellie, Ivory, Zuri, Emberly, and Judaya. You are beautiful and blessed!

To all the students I have taught in these past 27 years, thank you for letting me learn from you! I love to hear about your successes!

And to Sharon Huckaby, "Obie Jean," my friend since the 80s, who called me and vehemently said, "Syb, God wants you to write a book!"

Contents

CHAPTER ONE

A New Season

It was a Saturday afternoon in the spring of 1992. The kids were gone somewhere with friends, and I was at home cleaning the house. A tape played in the background. It was Christian Life College's men's quartet, and the song was "When Answers Aren't Enough." One of the verses says, "Instead of asking, 'why did it happen,' ask, 'where can it lead you from here?'" It was a message my soul needed to hear.

Our divorce was finalized on February 24 earlier that year. In the final agreement, I received the entire equity in our house, which was practically unheard of, especially because it was our only real asset. During the divorce process, I considered the idea of taking a few classes at Jackson College of Ministries. My daughter, Bethany, wanted to attend Bible college after graduation.

That spring day, as I was listening to that song, I began to think in a new direction concerning attending Bible college.

I could sell my house, and we could go now! My younger son, Grant, was graduating high school in May. My older son, Vance, was already married and living in Oklahoma. Excitement about my new season of life began to stir in me. I had faith! I could do this!

I had served as a musician and singer at my home churches ever since I received the Holy Ghost at age thirteen, but there was a lot about music I didn't know. My goal in going to college would be to learn more, so I could serve the Lord even better. I could focus all of my time and effort toward ministry and growing as a church musician.

First, I needed to talk to some people in my life—starting with my brother, Charles. Charles had been such a strength to me during the agonizing divorce. When I told him what I was thinking, I must have been pretty convincing because he simply said, "If you're going to change your life, you need to do it now!" He was referring, of course, to my age. I was almost 47.

I also talked to my pastor and some close friends before telling my son and daughter. Besides changing my life, this move would impact my children the most. Everyone for the most part was supportive.

In June, I placed our house on the market. I fully expected it to sell, so we could leave for Jackson, Mississippi in August. Unfortunately, it did not sell during those three months. We lived in a great neighborhood on a quiet dead-end street. The house was 2,800 square feet on a half-acre lot. The kids and I had lived there alone for five years, and the property was a bit rundown.

One night, we had gone to bed at about 11:00 p.m. as it started to rain. It wasn't long before hail began to pound the roof. I heard glass breaking, and suddenly felt cold water dripping on my face. It was the most severe hailstorm in the history of Arlington, Texas, up to that time.

Golf ball-sized hail damaged the roof and broke the large front windows in our home. Using the insurance money, I replaced the roof on the house and the detached garage, had the inside of the house painted, and hung new wallpaper in the kitchen and entryway.

At the end of August the house still had not sold, and I had to decide whether to renew the contract with the Realtor or to take the house off the market. After praying, I renewed the contract. I believed I had heard from God that we were to move. In September, I received an offer on the house. I countered, the buyers did too, and we finally settled on a price. It was at least $20,000 more than the house was thought to be worth at the time of the divorce.

Signing that contract to sell the house was like taking a big plunge into deep unknown waters. We would no longer have a roof over our heads, but we were headed for a big adventure! It was an exciting time to step out on faith!

In the meantime, that summer my son Grant acknowledged a call from God. He decided to attend Texas Bible College in Houston, which meant he would not be moving with us to Mississippi.

On the weekend before Christmas 1992, Bethany and I headed to Jackson, Mississippi to find a place to live. We didn't know anyone in the city, but trusted the Lord to guide us. I was driving a 1993 Chevrolet Lumina that I bought with the proceeds of the sale of the house. My last car had been a 1977 Dodge, so we felt like we had really stepped up in the world!

We did not know where to start looking for a place to live, so we decided to visit a church that Sunday and ask some of the members for some guidance. We visited the First Pentecostal Church on Sunday morning and started talking to the people there.

Someone recommended Homewood Manor Mobile Home Park on State Street, so I called the office on Monday morning. Sure enough, they had a two-bedroom trailer available. It was a far cry from the house I had just sold. The carpets were especially awful! Despite that, the rent was reasonable, and it was close to JCM, so I signed a lease that day. The next morning, I went downtown to pay the utility deposits and then we were on our way back to Texas. It was a quick work!

We celebrated Christmas with family and friends, enjoying the rest of the month. New Year's Eve was cold and filled with sleet and rain, but two men from my home church loaded our U-Haul that day. We were all set to leave the next morning.

My son, Vance, had flown in to help us drive the moving truck. Bethany and I took our cat, Cowboy, with us in the car. He meowed the entire way to Mississippi!

It was nearly dark when we arrived at our new home. We ate, quickly set up our beds, and went to sleep early. Tomorrow would be a busy day!

The next morning, we unloaded everything except for the washer and the piano—they were too heavy for us. That's when I went looking for David Henry, a JCM student. Someone at the church had told me that he and his wife Debbie lived in the mobile home park. Sure enough, he came to help unload the rest of our things. Debbie and Abigail, their little girl, came too. That evening I drove Vance to the airport in New Orleans and drove back to our new home in Jackson. We were all moved in.

The Henrys invited us over for lunch after church the next day. They ended up being our special blessing that first year and a half. David was a Junior at JCM, and Debbie was a scrub-tech at a local hospital. We spent a lot of time at their house. When we felt lonely or isolated, we could always walk down to Trailer #95.

In front of our trailer in Jackson, our first Easter

CHAPTER TWO

My Early Life

I was born about eight miles north of Silsbee, Texas, in a little community called Wiley May. I can't remember why it is called that, but our church was named the Wiley May Pentecostal Church.

I am the youngest of five children born to Harvey and Beatrice "Jolly" McNeely. I had three older sisters—Betty, Nelle, and Shirley—and one older brother, Charles.

My dad was a backslider at the time I was born and had been for a long time, but my mother was always in church and we kids attended church with her. I received the Holy Ghost at the age of 13 in a revival preached by Reverend Verbal Bean at the church in town. I had been baptized in Jesus' name when I was five.

Until I was a senior in high school, I always attended Silsbee Public Schools. During the summer before my senior year, the Lord spoke to my mother to move to Fort Worth. Of course, that would be a process, but I was able to move ahead of my parents because my sister Betty already lived there. It was quite a change from the small-town school I was used to. Mother and Daddy moved in January and we were reunited. I graduated from Polytechnic Senior High School in Fort Worth in 1963.

I got a job right out of high school as a typist and worked for a year. We had heard that Texas Bible College had opened in Houston in January of 1964, and I badly wanted to attend. I applied and was accepted for the fall semester. I only attended one year, but I fell in love with Bible College and all that it offered.

After returning home, I went to work again and was busy in our home church. My cousin, Reverend C. R. McNeely was the pastor. I taught Sunday School and was involved in the Music Department, singing and playing the piano or organ.

In 1967, my dad came back to church and lived for God for the rest of his life—another 18 years.

In 1968, I married, and we were blessed with three children—two sons, Vance and Grant, and one daughter, Bethany.

The Lord blessed us financially too, especially when my husband started his own plumbing company. The children all received the Holy Ghost and were baptized at young ages—the boys at six and Bethany at 7. We had a lot of things to be thankful for.

I lost both my parents fairly young. I was 29 when my Mother passed away. I think that was the hardest thing I had ever faced. My dad died in 1985. I was 40 years old.

Not long after, the next year in fact, my husband and I separated for a few months but then we reconciled. God had warned me about my marriage, but sometimes I have selective hearing.

During church one night, my brother told me I would walk through the "darkest valley" I had ever walked. I forgot what he told me until a friend reminded me when my marriage fell apart. I know I could not have stopped the process, but I might have been better prepared. The brokenness changed me, and for that I am eternally grateful.

Almost a year to the day of the first separation, my husband left again. This time he did not return. Looking back, I can see that there were always problems we should have addressed, but most marriages have them. I never expected to be a divorced woman. I just never thought it would happen to me. I was very immature. Despite my ignorance, God walked me through the process of healing from my divorce.

One of the first miracles I experienced came through the attorney the Lord provided for me. His name was Delbert Bartell. I first heard about him from a friend when I called to ask for a loan of $500 because my husband had filed for divorce, and I didn't have any money to hire a lawyer.

She told me that her co-worker had gotten a divorce, and she loved her lawyer, so she gave me his name. He didn't charge me anything to go and talk to him for the first time. If you know anything about attorneys, that just does not happen. I had previously talked to one and he charged me $75 for an hour of his time. All in all, Mr. Bartell only charged me a total of $400.

We went to the courthouse five times. The first time was for temporary orders. The second was about an air conditioner. The third time for disclosure. The fourth time we went was a busy day, and the judge did not get to us. On our fifth visit to the courthouse, the divorce was granted. That was when my ex-husband gave me all of the equity in the house—even the judge was not happy about that!

In the meantime, I was hired for a job at Halliburton Company and worked there for nearly five years. I started as a part-time "gopher" and ended up in the accounting department. I still have so many fond memories of the people I worked with there. It was during my fifth year at Halliburton that the hail storm happened and my story began.

Shades of things to come. Shirley and me with our first piano.

My siblings and me.
I'm the short 4 year old in front.

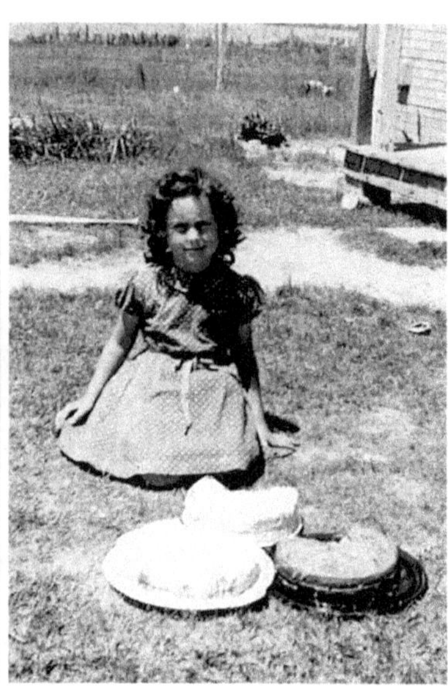

My seventh birthday.

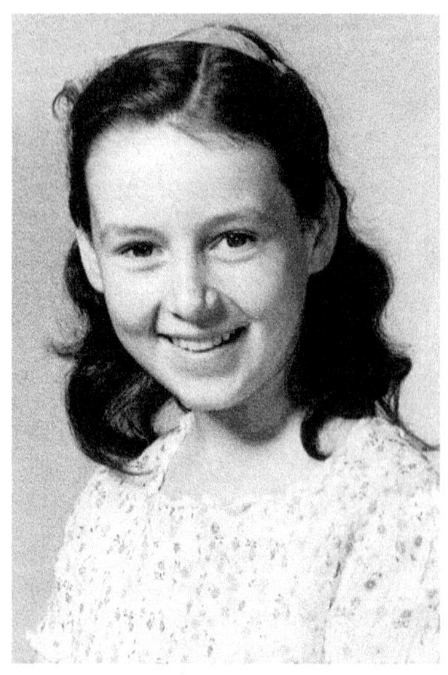

My 6th grade photo.

Age 15. Notice the bouffant skirt.

Our whole family after we moved to
Fort Worth. I'm on the far left.

My TBC student photo.

My children.
Vance 14, Grant 10, and Bethany, 6.

CHAPTER THREE

Life in Mississippi

Now that we were in Mississippi, it was harder in some ways than I had expected. In a practical sense, Mississippi and Texas cultures are quite different. It took at least a year before we began to feel at home.

Bethany and I both started school that January. She was in 9th grade, and I was a second-semester freshman at Jackson College of Ministries. At first, my fellow students didn't know what to think about this gray-haired lady who showed up to take classes with them, but they soon got used to me.

Meanwhile, I had to learn to study again. I had graduated Magna Cum Laude from high school and had one year of Texas Bible College behind me, but it had been a long time since I had seriously studied anything. I learned to read the material aloud so I would remember it better. Thankfully, I soon discovered I was not too old to learn! My grades were so good one student accused me of messing up the grade curve!

One plus about living in Jackson was the annual National Music Ministry Conference, known as NMMC. Every year that we lived in Jackson, we hosted a houseful of visitors from Texas for the conference. What fun we had, and it made us glad we moved to Mississippi!

When we first moved to Jackson, I saw a coffee table book about Abraham Lincoln in a bookstore at the mall. I have always enjoyed reading about Abraham Lincoln and I really wanted the book, but it was $50. I later saw it at WalMart for $37.50, but I still felt as if I couldn't pay that much for a book. One Wednesday night in July, I took my daughter to youth choir practice and drove over to K-Mart to look around as I waited for church to start.

K-Mart was having a sidewalk sale, which was mostly swim gear—beach balls, floats, and other stuff for the pool. I picked up a couple of things I didn't need and headed to the checkout counter. That's when I saw a lady standing there holding the

Lincoln book I wanted! She was casually flipping through it. I held my breath, praying she would lay the book down. When she did, I grabbed it. It had a 40 percent off sticker on it and was the only book in the sidewalk sale! I bought it for $15. It was such a small thing, but God knows ALL our wants. He knows exactly what we need at every moment.

Before we knew it, the first semester of school was over. Bethany and I had both done well. On Awards Day at her school, Bethany received seven certificates, two medals, and one trophy. I made all A's that first semester! We drove home to Texas for a visit, feeling triumphant, but two distressing events affected us that summer.

On the night of JCM's graduation, it was announced that the Dean of Music had resigned. Since he had established the Music Department there, no one knew what would happen now. As a music student, I was concerned.

The second event was the tragic death of one of Bethany's classmates. The untimely accident greatly saddened us. The girl was only 16-years-old. She was a lovely, multi-talented young lady. The entire congregation at the church we attended, JCM, and Bethany's school were all impacted by the young girl's death.

I felt shaken and unsure of our situation. I just needed to hear from the Lord again, to be sure that I was where He wanted me to be. I began to ask Him to let me know that I was still in His will by staying in Jackson.

Camp Meeting in Mississippi is in July. On the third night after the service, I had a dream. In the dream, I was talking to my Aunt Ruby who had died about a year before. I told her I had always loved her. She replied, "I know you do." Then an unusual thing happened. She pointed her finger at me, and it grew longer and began to glow. She said, "I've thought about you all day today. The Lord will hold many doors open for you. You will go back on your word once, but not twice."

Suddenly, I was wide awake. I knew the Lord had spoken to me. He had answered my prayer. I didn't understand how His will would come to pass, about the "doors" that would open. I didn't know how I would go back on my word, but I knew I had heard from God, and that was what mattered. He knew my situation, and I was at peace.

By the time August rolled around, I needed to find a job. We had been living on child support and the money we made from the sale of the house. I had worked at a few temporary jobs but needed something permanent.

Someone told me that the pastor's brother could probably help me find a job, so I called him. He hired me to work in the operations center of the bank where he was a Vice President. I worked Thursday through Saturday nights from 4 p.m. until midnight. It worked pretty well with my school schedule since classes started at 7:50 a.m. and ended around 1 p.m.

I worked at the bank for two years. The next summer, I had a better work schedule. I worked from 1 p.m. to 6 p.m. It was a great job for a Bible college student, and it helped me not to spend all my savings.

CHAPTER FOUR

Changes

In the fall of 1993, I took a heavy load of classes. I was a semester behind even though I did not plan to graduate. We became more involved at church, singing in the adult and youth choirs, and going to prayer meetings, and other events. Bethany got her driver's license, and my younger son was married!

The Music Department at JCM continued on. Lisa Gimnich, one of the teachers from the previous year, was the new Dean of Music at JCM. Sadly, the overall enrollment at the school took a nosedive, but I knew I was supposed to continue attending.

I received a great compliment when the Music Club elected me as the Treasurer. It meant more work because the responsibilities included overseeing music conference registration, but it was still an honor.

While working on the registration with a senior music major, I confided that I might not come back in the fall. She looked me in the eye and said emphatically, "You need to graduate!"

Her words went right to my heart; she was right. Besides, where would we go? We had no home to go back to. That settled it. We would stay another year, and by adding in correspondence and taking some CLEP tests, maybe I could graduate that next spring.

The summer of 1994 was eventful in several ways. The Henrys moved after David graduated. Their absence left a huge hole in our lives. A classmate of mine stayed with us for the summer. She had a job but no car, so we taxied her back and forth.

My older son Vance and his wife moved to Jackson and stayed with us in our two-bedroom trailer. They brought their dog along too! Since we had a cat, and with so many people living together, it made for an interesting dynamic in the Bowman household.

Then we heard word that our new Dean of Music was leaving after just one year. We were back to square one for the Music Department. I had no idea what would happen next, but I continued to trust the Lord.

All of the challenges we faced that summer were offset by some good news we received in August. Brother and Sister Bret Cooley were coming to JCM! He would serve as the Dean of Missions and she would be the new Dean of Music! Dedie Cooley was well-known for her outstanding musical abilities. We were so excited!

I was a senior that fall when Sister Cooley became our Dean of Music. She was the instructor for my keyboard and conducting classes. I also took private piano lessons from her for one semester. I learned so much from Sister Cooley.

One day in late September, the music office secretary asked me if I could go to Vicksburg for the weekend to play the organ for their church services. The pastor, Brother Tipton, had called the school looking for a musician. So, on Sunday morning, Bethany and I set out for Vicksburg, which was about a 45-minute drive. We spent the day there, and I played the music for both services. At the end of the day, they gave me a check for $100! I had never been paid to play music for church before! I had no idea, but that was the start of God opening a door for me.

CHAPTER FIVE

Graduation

Sister Wolfe gave us an assignment in Music Composition class. We were to write a country or southern Gospel song. I tried for several days, but I just felt hopeless. Then on the Sunday night before the song was due the next Tuesday, I was inspired by the title of the sermon that was preached: "Shift Change in Heaven." The title of that sermon triggered a memory of a message my son Vance preached called, "God Works the Night Shift." I sat there in church, took an index card out of my purse, and began to write.

The lyrics started with the line: "It was after midnight when I came to my wit's end." When I arrived back home after church, I asked Vance to remind me of the examples he used when he preached his sermon. One of them was about Peter being delivered from prison, so I decided to use that one in my song. I continued to work on the song the next day. By Monday evening, I had finished writing my song and shared it with a couple of classmates.

When I arrived at class the next day, Sister Wolfe said we didn't have to turn our songs in. She only wanted us to write "God-inspired" songs! I felt disappointed after all of the work I had done and just sat there after class was dismissed. That's when a fellow student came to me and said, "I heard about the song you wrote. Come to the piano and sing it."

After a little urging, I did. Sister Wolfe stopped talking to the other students, came over to where I was, and listened. She said, "I like that song!" That moment triggered a series of events.

Sister Wolfe told Sister Cooley about my song. Sister Cooley told the JCM Quartet about it. Everyone liked the song, and the Quartet ended up recording it on their CD!

Three and a half years before, the Lord had given me a message through my pastor. The message was if I would continue in the direction I was going, not turning to the right or left, God would do things in my life that I could not imagine. The open door with my song surely had to be one of those things God was doing!

In January of 1995, Brother Tipton, the pastor from the Vicksburg church where I had played the organ that one Sunday in October came to teach classes at JCM. When I met him, I let him know if he ever needed a musician again, I was available. Sure enough, one day in March, he asked me to come to their church to play music the following Sunday.

We all went, my daughter, son, and daughter-in-law, and we all participated. I sang. Dana sang. We both sang with Bethany, and Vance testified. The church service was awesome! After church, Brother Tipton gave me a check and asked me to pray about coming to serve at the Vicksburg church after I graduated!

Sister Cooley and I had talked about this very thing. Since my daughter had only one more year of high school, I didn't want to move her again. Sister Cooley said, "Wouldn't it be great if there was a church within driving distance of Jackson where you could become the music director?"

Vicksburg was the ideal place. It was 47 miles from our house to the church. Still, I wanted to be sure I was in God's will, so I waited and prayed. Besides that, I hadn't even graduated from JCM yet.

The 20th anniversary of NMMC was in 1995. It was a wonderful conference. We had a houseful of visitors, as usual. Sadly, we also had a funeral.

A fellow senior music major died right before the conference. He was the other "older" student in my class, still a lot younger than me, but older than most of the students. His name was Ron Wesley. He was 33 years old when he died and left behind a wife and two children.

Graduation was set for May 19, 1995, and we had a family dilemma. My son Grant was graduating the exact same night from Texas Bible College. As a mother, I had a difficult decision to make. Grant was the practical one. He said, "Mom, you graduate, and I'll graduate, and we'll celebrate together later!" So, it was decided, but it was bittersweet for both of us.

I finished all my correspondence and classes and was ready to graduate. On my 50th birthday, my class left for our senior trip. We went to Orlando for a week and returned in time for the end-of-year banquet. When it was over, the Academic Dean approached me and said, "You need to prepare a speech for tomorrow night. Your grade point average is 3.94, and you are this year's salutatorian!" I was beyond excited!

Several family members and friends came to see me graduate. It was a happy and emotional night. Vance helped me with my speech. I started by saying that when I was expecting my daughter, my hair was already turning gray, and someone asked if I was too old to have a baby! Someone else replied, "Evidently not!"

When I came to JCM, I asked myself, "Am I too old to learn? Evidently not!" That got a laugh or two. Then I quoted Isaiah 43:18-19. "Remember ye not the former things, neither consider the things of old. Behold, I will do a new thing . . ."

I finished by talking to the class of 1995 about the changes we had all seen at the college in the three years we had been there. We had three Deans—one each for Theology, Missions, and Music. I talked about how each person had enriched my life and said, "Don't forget to remember, if it becomes very dark in your life, God works the night shift!"

My 50th birthday with my kids.

My graduating class 1995, Jackson College of Ministries. I was 50.

CHAPTER SIX

A Place to Labor

At the end of Bethany's school year, she was awarded as the MVP in volleyball. She was always more athletic than her mom! My son Grant and his wife Kellie were expecting their first baby—my first grandchild—later that year in October. I wanted to make sure I kept my family as a priority in my life. I didn't want to become so overly committed that my family suffered.

By the middle of June, Brother Tipton and I had talked again and had come up with a plan. He wanted me to come to Vicksburg to play the piano every Sunday and Wednesday when I could make it, and to coordinate special singing. He would give me an offering every time I came. I felt really good about the freedom of our arrangement.

In the meantime, I only had a part-time job. I had graduated college and was having to dip into my savings pretty often, which bothered me.

Thankfully, God had another door ready to swing open that I was not aware of.

Like I said before, camp meeting in Mississippi is always in July. The morning session started at 10 a.m. with two preachers. The Bible lesson started at 12:30. I left around that time to go to work at the bank. On Thursday, I asked my supervisor if I could come in to work later on Friday so I could stay to listen to the last Bible lesson at camp. She said yes.

I was sitting by myself at the camp meeting when Brother and Sister Craft walked in and sat next to me, leaving one empty chair between us. Brother Craft was the president of JCM at that time. When 1:30 p.m. came around, I leaned over to tell them goodbye. Brother Craft got up, moved around his wife, and sat down next to me.

He said, "Do you think that maybe you could teach some of the classes at JCM?"

I said, "Yes!" I was not at all certain how confidently I actually could teach those classes, but I knew something special had just happened. A door had just opened for me.

In October of 1995, I became a grandmother when Kaylie Paige Bowman was born to my son Grant and his wife Kellie. She was beautiful! My life was becoming more and more full, and I felt great about the doors God had opened for me.

The next four years were very busy and passed quickly. We loved the church at Vicksburg, and I loved teaching at JCM! I learned so much at both places and enjoyed the best of both worlds—church and Bible college.

Some of the most powerful and anointed services I have ever been in happened in Vicksburg, Mississippi. Brother Tipton was a wonderful pastor with a great sense of humor, as well as a seriousness about the things of God. He had an exceptional ability to walk in the Spirit.

One day, I was in his office at the college when he said to me, "You know, I think that being around all these young people at college slows the aging process!" I thought about that for a while.

I was 51 at the time and thought I could see myself as possibly being somewhat younger than my actual age, so I decided to give myself some extra years! Five years didn't seem to be long enough. Ten years seemed to be too long, so I finally decided that seven was a good number for me to settle on. And, since the college students "slowed the aging process," instead of being 51, I could think of myself as 44! I think the Lord agreed with me!

Many times, Brother Tipton would walk to the pulpit and begin to speak a word from the Lord. The gifts of the Spirit were very much evident in that church. Vance and Dana ended up moving to Vicksburg and became the youth leaders at the church. We all grew spiritually while we were there.

My family at the JCM Christmas Banquet my first year of teaching. Kaylie is the baby

CHAPTER SEVEN

Adventure in Africa

After Bethany graduated from Jackson Christian Academy in May of 1996, I surprised all of us—even myself—by telling my family I was planning a trip to Africa that summer! It had been on my mind for a while. Our friends, the Halls, were missionaries in Kenya and had asked Bethany and me to come and visit. I still had some money left from the sale of the house and decided if I was ever going to go, it needed to be now!

My pastor approved my time off for the trip and the Lord provided someone to take care of the music while we were gone. We flew out from Houston on Sunday afternoon, July 7, and arrived in London at 7 a.m. on the 8th. As I looked down at the coastline of England from the airplane, tears filled my eyes. Surely this had to be another one of those God-things I could not imagine.

I booked a day tour of London, and when we arrived at Gatwick Airport I had no time to rent a locker to store our carry-on bags and pillows. We had to find the tour booth and hurry to the train that went to Victoria Station, where we were met by a representative of the tour. We visited Westminster Abbey, watched the changing of the guard at Buckingham Palace, had lunch during a boat ride on the Thames River, and toured St. Paul's Cathedral and the Tower of London.

A funny thing happened at the end of the tour. One of our friends suggested that we visit the Hard Rock Café since the original one is in London. When the bus headed back to the train station, I asked our tour guide if he knew where the Hard Rock Café was. He said no, but the bus driver knew where to let us off so that we could take a city bus there.

We exited the tour bus in that city of 8 million people holding our carry-on luggage and pillows, and waited at a bus stop for either Bus 7, 14, or 2. Sure enough, a bus with one of those numbers came along and we boarded. I told that bus driver we wanted to go to the Hard Rock Café, but he said he didn't know where it was.

Praise the Lord, a couple getting on the bus behind us told us they knew where it was and would tell us what stop to get off at. When it was time for us to exit, the couple pointed us in the right direction.

"Do you see that white building over there? The Hard Rock Café is near there."

It was across eight lanes of traffic, but thankfully there was a subway-sort of a tunnel running under the street. After walking down and then back up, we found the white building the couple had mentioned and asked for directions.

"Walk outside and go left. It's right down the street."

Sure enough, we found the restaurant and a line of tourists waiting for tables. When we finally made it up to the host, he happened to be an American. Looking us over, and eying our baggage, especially our pillows, he smiled and asked, "How long are you planning to stay?"

After eating, we had to get back to Victoria Station, and by that time it was dark. We needed a taxi, so I began to try to flag one down, but it didn't work as I had hoped. I didn't know how to whistle loudly. Finally, a taxi pulled up to let someone out, and I ran over and asked if he could take us to Victoria Station. I told him I only had five pounds of English money left. He said that would be enough, so we made it back in time to catch the train to the airport.

Our flight left London at 10:30 p.m. and we arrived in Nairobi, Kenya, around 9 a.m. on July 9th. Talk about jet lag! My friend Patricia Hall let us sleep awhile but then woke us up to help us adjust to the time change. In a few days, we were fine.

Oh, the sights we saw! We visited four safari parks to see the "big five" animals—lions, leopards, elephants, rhinoceroses, and cape buffalo, shopped in the markets, and saw the Rift Valley. We went to church, met some wonderful saints of God, and played games with the Halls at night.

We bought fruit from roadside stands. We went to the equator and watched a demonstration of water as it was poured down a funnel. On one side of the equator, the water swirled to the right, on the other side, it swirled to the left, but right on top of the equator, the water went straight down. It may have been a staged demonstration, but it was a fun experience, nonetheless.

We stayed in Kenya for three and a half weeks. God is awesome to allow us to see so much of His creation!

At the Aberdare Country Club, Kenya, Africa

Eating with the Wards from Tanzania, and the Halls from Kenya.

First Sunday in Nairobi, Kenya, Lunch time!

At the Equator in Kenya, Africa, with Sis. Hall's nephew, Eric Dunlap.

CHAPTER EIGHT

The Last Laugh

When we arrived back home from Africa, there had been some changes. Vance and Dana had moved to Vicksburg. They now lived in a double-wide behind the church, and our pastor had been appointed as the Vice President of JCM!

It was my second year to teach, and this time Sister Cooley entrusted me with a few of the more advanced classes. I guess I was getting a little better!

Bethany enrolled as a freshman at JCM that fall. She had turned 18 while we were in Africa. Because I was an instructor at the college, Bethany's tuition was free. She had applied for and received a scholarship from the UPC Department of Education, which would pay for her books. That was another one of those things I could not imagine happening! Bethany completed the three-year music program and her education was free! She also had some of the best teachers in existence. What a blessing!

General Conference was in San Antonio in 1996, and we were able to attend. We saw a lot of people we knew and had a mini family reunion since all of my children were there.

In December, we made our usual trek to Texas for the holidays. In January, it was back to school. In March, the music conference brought Texas visitors to stay with us for the fifth year in a row. That month, we also had an unusual church service in Vicksburg, which lasted for four hours!

One of the senior music majors had come to teach a choir clinic that day, and it was great. Someone received the Holy Ghost, and Brother Tipton dismissed the service. Suddenly, three people gave messages in tongues, and Brother Tipton interpreted the messages, telling us it was worship that brought the Lord's glory down and it was worship that would retain His glory!

We all started praying for each other and some of us began laughing in the Spirit. I felt led to testify about how the devil had laughed at me because my marriage was destroyed, but that I had two sons, two daughters-in-law, and one daughter who were all serving the Lord. I was having the last laugh after all! The devil also tried to tell me I had made a mistake by selling my home and moving to Mississippi, but there was a revival there, and I was still laughing! Several others testified as well, and we all left exhausted, but very happy and full of joy!

CHAPTER NINE

Health & Happiness

In May of 1997, Zachary Vance Bowman—my second grandchild and first grandson—joined our family. Vance and Dana were the proud parents and I fell in love with him right away. Bethany finished her first year of JCM and I finished my second year as an instructor there.

I was having a little car trouble and had already had to replace the alternator and battery in my car once. In June, the car started losing power again. On the advice of someone at a car parts store, I replaced the battery and thought the problem was solved, but Wednesday night on our way home to Jackson from church in Vicksburg, the car died right before the exit to take us to the north side of town. I had to decide quickly whether to exit or continue down I-20. I decided on the latter.

About a hundred yards further was the exit sign for Ellis Avenue. The exit was still another 1 and

1/4 miles away. We were still moving, though we had no power whatsoever. I tapped the brake, but Gena said, "Don't hit the brake, Sister Bowman!"

We coasted all the way to Ellis Avenue and all the way down the exit ramp where we finally rolled to a stop. Back then, no one had cell phones. We walked to a nearby station and called a friend who sent someone to pick us up and take us home. The next day, we went to get the car and take it to the shop.

I don't know anything about the law of physics, but I would venture to say that it is nearly impossible for a car to coast over a mile after losing power. I could just picture an angel at the back of the car giving us a push.

For Christmas that year, we performed a musical at the church in Vicksburg called, "He Came to Us," written by Wayne and Elizabeth Goodine. It was the first time I had been in charge of a musical production. With some help from my daughter and her friends, about twelve singers, and a few actors, we pulled it off. Brother Tipton said it was awesome!

In January of 1998, grandson number two was born to Grant and Kellie. His name is Kendall Grant Bowman. The doctor had told Grant and Kellie the baby was a girl and even declared that he would bet anything except his wife and dog that the baby was a girl! Obviously, he was dead wrong! Early in the morning of January 22, Kendall was born by C-section. Grant was so surprised the baby was a boy that he turned white and had to sit down!

Several things of significance happened in 1998. That summer, Bethany went to a small church to lead music. She trained someone else to play the piano after she was gone. I taught a choir clinic for the first time that summer.

Sister Cooley resigned as Dean of Music. All the music majors took her resignation hard, and so did I. She had been my teacher for one year and my boss for three. She stayed one more year to teach, so we were glad about that!

My brother Charles had a 15-hour surgery for a brain tumor, and the Lord brought him through. Thankfully, the tumor was benign.

I found a lump in my breast around the same time, and the Lord walked me through the process so gently and purposefully. I was so scared. I called my doctor back in Arlington, Texas, who had delivered my children. His nurse, whom I had known for years, tried to be reassuring but urged me to see a doctor in Jackson ASAP.

I went to Dr. Sullivan, Dana's doctor. She wanted me to have a radiological mammogram right away but said that we could wait as long as two months. I talked to my kids, and they didn't think I should put it off. I also talked to my pastor's wife, and her advice was the same. When I called Dr. Sullivan back to tell her, she said I had been on her mind and that we would both sleep better if we went ahead and made the appointment.

I was still very concerned—well, worried is probably the right word. The very same evening a lady knocked on my trailer door. She was looking for someone else, but after talking for a few minutes, I invited her in. For some reason, I felt like confiding in her about the lump I had found. She happened to be a nurse who worked in radiology! She reassured me about the negligible effects of mammograms and stressed the need for haste.

On the Wednesday evening before the test, I called my brother. As soon as he picked up the phone, he asked, "What's up with you?" I explained my situation. He told me not to worry. He said that one thing he had learned from having the brain tumor is that we worry about the state of our bodies too much and not enough about our spiritual state.

At church that night, the young preacher asked for people who had a need to step out in the aisle as an act of faith. He said the Lord would meet our needs if we would step out. I walked all the way to the front of the church. My pastor prayed briefly for me and then moved on to pray for others.

Then there was a message in tongues. When it was interpreted it was almost verbatim to what my brother had told me. The Lord said He was more concerned about our spirits and souls than our bodies, but He had ministered to us and touched our spirits, souls, and bodies! I knew He had touched me in that moment, and I had peace.

During the time of prayer, I had a sensation of being surrounded. I thought the ladies of the church had gathered around me to pray for me, but when I opened my eyes there were only four of us at the front. I can only surmise that the angels had encompassed me.

When I went for the ultrasound, the technician said, "Well, it's a cyst just like we hoped it would be."

I said, "The Lord already told me on Wednesday night that it was going to be okay, but it is nice to hear you confirm it!" Later, I had the cyst aspirated.

When school started again, JCM had a new Dean of Music, Sister Juanita Clark. Quite unexpectedly, she gave me a small group to oversee—JCM's Men's Quartet. I was so surprised and honored. I was allowed to pick all the singers and musicians.

We had so much fun. We practiced every Tuesday during lunch, which was our day to fast, and we had the opportunity to sing quite a few times during the school year. The greatest honor we had was opening for the Crabb Family at a concert in Pearl, Mississippi. We met the entire group, but the friendliest of all of them was Jason Crabb. What a nice person he is! Those were exciting times!

Every year, JCM held a Missions Conference and that year Brother Bruce Howell was the special speaker. On the last night, as we gathered around to pray, he came to me and told me, "God's gonna take care of those two things that you are concerned about."

I knew exactly what two things he was talking about. I needed to know whether this would be my last year at JCM, and I was also concerned for my daughter. This was her last year in college. She would graduate in May, and I didn't know what the future held for her. Where would we go from here?

The JCM Quartet and me, 1998-99.

CHAPTER TEN

Back to Texas

January began my last semester at JCM, though I didn't know it would be my last when it started. It was odd that I was only asked to teach four hours per week, and was off on Monday, Wednesday, and Friday. In my journal, I wrote, "Lord, are you trying to tell me something?"

Vance and Dana had already left Vicksburg in the summer of 1998 to evangelize, and in March of 1999, they took the pastorate of the United Pentecostal Church of Shawnee, Oklahoma, where they still pastor.

On a Sunday night in February, my friend Heather told me about a dream she had about me. In the dream, I was sitting at the organ, and she was standing nearby ready to help me sing. I looked at her I said, "Heather, I'm gonna sing Amazing Grace."

She replied, "Go ahead, if that's what you feel."

When she looked out at the church, some of the people were laughing and making fun, but the Lord began to move, and people responded. I knew the dream was significant but didn't know exactly how.

From time to time in the coming months, Heather and I would talk it over. We finally concluded that the dream was about a decision that I would make that most people would not understand or agree with, but it would turn out to be the right decision.

In April, the Dean of Music asked me to pray about moving out of my office, and into a little cubbyhole in another building. I'm not really into prestige, but the move felt like another sign that the Lord was pulling me away from JCM. Heather's husband Mark later confirmed what I was feeling.

Where would I go? I had sold my house in Texas, so I couldn't go back to Arlington. I also had to have a job, or did I?

In April, my sister called me. She lived in Brookeland, Texas, which is a very small town in East Texas not far from Louisiana. They were having a revival and the evangelist had given his testimony. He had been backslidden, and the

Lord used the song "Amazing Grace" to draw him back. As we were talking, I remembered Heather's dream and that the song was the same. During the conversation, we felt the Lord's presence, and my sister asked me to come and visit during the revival.

The very next weekend, I went to Brookeland for a visit. On Sunday morning, the pastor asked me to sing. After I sang, the evangelist got up to preach. He said that I would be a part of the revival at the church, and would be there for an interim period of time. I didn't understand the prophecy at all, and after church, I asked him what he had meant. He said he did not know but had said what he felt led to say in the Holy Ghost.

I went home to Jackson and began making plans to move to Brookeland, Texas. My daughter graduated in May and we went on vacation at Disney World. Bethany was going to move to Oklahoma to be the music director at Vance's church.

By June 8th, I was living with my sister in the woods of East Texas. It was very quiet. After living in a large city, being involved at the Bible College, where there is always something going on, and being a part of the wonderful church in Vicksburg, I had a hard time adapting to the slower pace.

At least we had the excitement of the revival, which went on until sometime in August! Quite a few people received the Holy Ghost, about 100 in all.

In September, I started teaching piano lessons. I had no income and my savings from the sale of the house were dwindling. By word of mouth, I had about ten piano students. I also taught my sister who had always wanted to be able to play in church. Of course, I didn't charge her! I also taught a choir clinic in Arlington, Texas, which gave me some earnings.

In October, I went to Oklahoma to see Vance and Dana and we went to Oklahoma City to hear Brother Larry Booker preach. "What Will Become of Your Dreams?" was the title of his message. It felt like he was preaching directly to me. He said that Joseph could have given in to despair, but instead, he made the best of whatever situation he found himself in. He probably had the cleanest cell in the prison!

How I needed that message. I went back to Brookeland determined to do my best there. We put on a Christmas musical, and I taught the pastor's wife to sing alto. We performed special songs and learned new choruses.

On December 16, Zathan Cole Bowman was born to Vance and Dana. He was grandson number three. What an auburn-haired cutie! And then there were four—grandkids, that is!

My friend Heather and me. We have been friends since our JCM days.

Bunaland

In February of 2000, I received an opportunity to go to Georgia to try out for a music director's position. Even though I decided not to take the offer, it was nice to know that a pastor wanted me. After all, I was almost 55!

In the meantime, I had met a new friend—Stephanie Clenney. She was a pastor's wife and had started a Sectional Youth Choir. She asked me to help, and I gladly accepted. It was through this opportunity that the next door would open for me.

At ladies' conference that year, my pastor's wife from the church in Arlington, Sister Harris, told me that she felt a door would open soon. Sister Jeffcoat, another pastor's wife I knew, told me the same thing. In my experience, God always confirms His word.

Sure enough, after the Sectional Youth Choir sang at a youth rally, I received a call from Brother Gary Sylvester who pastored in Buna, Texas. He asked if I was interested in coming to be their music director. He offered housing and a salary and suggested I come for a try-out weekend. I did and I enjoyed myself very much. He and his wife Becky treated me so well and restated their offer for me to come there.

On May 12, 2000, I got word that my son Vance had been in a serious car accident while attending a ministers' conference in Dallas. He had been riding in the car with three other young ministers and was seated behind the driver. That is where the other vehicle struck them. The impact turned their car completely around and then they were hit on the opposite side of their car.

He received a concussion and loss of memory for a few hours. That night, Brother Wayne McClain came to one of the hotel rooms where they were staying and told them that the devil tried to kill all of them because of the ministries that were represented in that one car. Thank the Lord they were protected by His hand.

I decided to take the music minister position in Buna for a trial period of three months, and on June 10, I moved into the evangelists' quarters at the church, which consisted of a bedroom, a kitchen with an eat-in dining room, and a bathroom.

After the three-month trial, I was offered a permanent position and given the option of moving into the church parsonage, which was next door to the church. It was a three-bedroom house with two bathrooms. I decided against the house but said "yes" to taking the position.

I was in charge of the chorale, which had about twenty members, and I played the keyboard for church along with Sister Sylvester who was a great organist. She picked the worship set and altar songs, which was wonderful because I have never been great at selecting songs!

In the five years that I stayed there—yes, five years—I did a lot more! I was in charge of the special programs for Mother's Day and Father's Day, scheduled special songs for nearly every service, sang in a ladies' trio, helped with two kids' Christmas musicals, and directed the chorale at community services at different denominal churches, which was one of the BEST things! We held a choir concert at the church, and I was over music scheduling at a huge fundraiser event called Extravaganza. I was so glad I had all of my Vicksburg experience to guide me.

In the execution of all these activities, I had a great sidekick! The Sylvester's grandson, Ryan, was a teenager then and had a flair for drama, which was good because I certainly did not! He helped with all the dramas and musicals and was a great blessing to me.

One of the first people I met when I arrived in Buna was a lady named Sue Roberts. As I said before, I was living in the church's evangelist quarters, and she happened to be cleaning the church at that time, so we struck up a conversation out in the hallway. We discovered that I knew a couple of her siblings as I was growing up in Silsbee, which was nearby. She knew some members of my family too. In fact, my cousin, Roy McNeely, had performed the ceremony when she and her husband Larry married.

Like most mothers, we had to do a little bragging about our kids. She told me about her son Chad, who had just completed his first year at Texas Bible College in Houston and was currently in Bolivia on a mission trip. I proceeded to tell her about my daughter Bethany who had graduated from Jackson College of Ministries and was currently the music director at her brother's church in Oklahoma. We decided somehow they should meet each other! How's that for matchmaking?

It was several more months before the introduction took place. About five months later, on the Sunday after Thanksgiving, they finally met. Nine months after they first met, almost to the day, on August 25, 2001, the wedding was in Buna. My daughter, Bethany Suzanne Bowman, married Chad Evan Roberts. It is their story to tell, but they have pastored in both Marshall and Midlothian, Texas, and Chad has served as the Secretary of the Texas District. They have four gorgeous children: Miranda, Evan, Colin, and Mason. Sue and I did good!

CHAPTER TWELVE

God's Provision for my Health

The last year I lived in Jackson, I had a couple of gallbladder attacks. At first, I didn't realize what was happening, but after talking to different people, I was pretty sure I knew. I didn't know what to do about it. I had no health insurance and couldn't afford to buy any. After moving back to Texas, I had a few more attacks in Brookeland, especially after high-fat meals, but by the next morning, I felt fine.

I had been living in Buna only a couple of months when one Sunday night after church I had the most severe gallbladder attack ever. I called the Sylvesters to come and pray for me. The pain subsided some, but unlike the previous times it never completely went away. I decided I was ready to go to the hospital, insurance or not, so the next morning Sister Sylvester took me to St. Elizabeth's

Hospital in Beaumont. We waited several hours in the emergency room before they finally took me back and gave me something for the pain.

An ultrasound confirmed that I had gallstones, and bloodwork showed my liver enzymes were elevated. Around 9 p.m. they put me in a room, and a very tired Sister Sylvester finally went home.

The next morning when the doctor came to see me, I was sure he would recommend surgery, but to my surprise, he told me I could control the symptoms by changing my diet and that surgery would be very expensive. There was a problem with his diagnosis, though. That very morning, the hospital had served me crispy rice and 2% milk for breakfast. After I ate, the pain began. I told the doctor I believed he was wrong. He recommended that I go to the ER in Galveston at UTMB. He said they would keep me there and perform the surgery.

Very early on Thursday morning, three ladies from the church took me to Galveston. Sure enough, they admitted me and performed the operation on Monday morning. In the meantime, I had developed pancreatitis. On Wednesday after the surgery, they did a scope procedure to check for more stones in the bile duct. It was a horrible experience because I woke up during the procedure. They removed some "sludge," but I was still very sick. I developed a metallic taste in my mouth. I wasn't allowed to eat, and sometimes not even allowed to drink.

Finally, it was Monday again, a week after the surgery. I was not well, and the doctors decided another scope procedure was necessary. This one was not so bad, as I did not wake up, but they couldn't find anything and decided I should go home. I was still not well. My bilirubin and enzymes were too high, but they couldn't do anything about it. I had stayed at the hospital two full weeks. What should have been a routine procedure turned into something worse.

When I got the final bill it was $39,000!

And remember the overnight stay at the hospital in Beaumont? The bill for that was $2,600! I now found myself in debt for nearly $42,000, with very limited means to pay it back.

The good news was that I did gradually get better, and in a few weeks, I felt like my old self again. The better news is that God had a plan to take care of the debt. I had requested financial assistance forms from both hospitals, filled them out, and sent them back.

While I was waiting to hear from them, two things happened that were beyond coincidence. First, I heard from my good friend Patricia Hall about a mission conference in Livingston, Texas, where some friends would be ministering, including the Halls. I decided to go not only for the joy of being with them but for the opportunity to make something right.

One of the missionaries there was Robert Harris. His dad had been my pastor in Arlington before I went to JCM. He was one of the two men who had loaded the U-Haul trailer for me on that sleet-filled day in December of 1992 so I could move to Mississippi. For eight years, I regretted not paying those guys! After years of struggling, I had some money in the bank as I had just sold my house, but I didn't give them anything except a thank you. It bothered me ever since. Now, it was time to do the right thing.

It seemed the Lord was testing me to see what I would do. I didn't have a lot of that money left and I didn't know if God would help me with my hospital bills or not, but even if He didn't, I knew what I had to do. On Saturday, October 14, 2000, I finally paid the debt I owed to Rob Harris.

Four days later, I was getting dressed for Wednesday night service when someone knocked on my door. It was a couple looking for Brother Sylvester. Their last name was Hutchison. They were from Louisiana, and he was going to preach that night.

I told them Brother Sylvester was probably in the prayer room. He looked at me kind of funny and said, "I think I've met you before. Did you ever attend Brother Craft's church in Jackson, Mississippi?" Of course I had, and then it dawned on me.

In 1994, there was another situation where two men had done me a service, and I had failed again to compensate them for it. I am a slow learner! I bought a storage building and needed someone to move it across the street, around the fence and the tree, and park it at the end of my trailer. Single women always seem to need help! Did I mention that it was the middle of a hot, muggy August? That the storage building was homemade, heavy, and not on wheels? The street was on an incline and it took them three or four hours to accomplish the feat.

The man standing at my door with his wife was one of the men who had helped me. How had he gotten to Buna, Texas? It seems that a minister friend had called in a favor to Brother Sylvester and asked him if Brother Hutchison could preach for him. As far as I know, it is the only time he ever ministered in Buna, but God's timing is amazing! It was an opportunity for me to right another wrong. So, I did.

Three days later, I received a letter from the Beaumont hospital. They had approved my request for financial aid, and my account balance was zero! Less than a month later, I heard from Galveston. They had forgiven my debt of $39,000! It was a God-orchestrated miracle.

Something else happened the following summer, which was further proof of the Lord's great care for me. My doctor found a knot on the left side of my abdomen and made me a rush appointment at the hospital in Galveston where I had gone to have my gallbladder removed.

The doctor seemed very concerned about the knot, but when I arrived at the hospital, they could not find a knot on my left side. They did say that I needed hernia surgery and scheduled it for a few months later. After the surgery, while I was in recovery, an unusual thing happened. I asked about the hernia and they said they only found two, one above the navel and one on my right side, but they had found nothing on my left side.

I'm happy to say that since then I have had no more abdominal surgeries! I think the doctor finding that knot was just the Lord's way of taking care of me—again!

CHAPTER THIRTEEN

Answered Prayers

I made some good friends while living with my sister in Brookeland, Bob and Connie Martin. I taught her piano lessons and spent quite a lot of time with them. One night when I was frustrated with my situation and was expressing it to them, Bob gave me a scripture—Proverbs 4:11-12. He also challenged me to go to the church every morning to pray. I prayed that scripture over and over.

After I had prayed over that scripture for several weeks, the Lord opened the door for me to go to Buna. We have to knock if we want God to open a door!

The Martins were friends with Sister Lois George, a lady minister. I had never met her, and she has since passed away, but at their request, she prayed for me over the phone. The prayer took place around Christmas of 2000.

I had only been in for Buna six months but felt there was something more the Lord wanted me to do. Sister George confirmed that with a word from the Lord. She told me to wait on Him, to be prayerful, to stay humble, and to guard my spirit. He had "a work" for me and it was not far away.

Her prophecy confirmed what Brother Cecil Sullivan had prophesied to me back in July. It was a long prophecy, but the gist was: "There's a place you're supposed to be working. There's a place you're supposed to be going. There's a thing you're supposed to be doing. You've got a ministry, sister."

Brother Jeff Faris also gave me a word several months later in 2001. He said, "You have no idea how the Lord is gonna use you in the last days, but you've had a glimpse so, let it flow!"

All of these words from the Lord were preparing me for the next door. I didn't know how it would all come together, I just knew that there was a longing inside of me, and I wanted to do all and be all the Lord desired.

I thought I might be a missionary since I was connected to so many missionaries. I sent off for an Associate in Missions "AIM" application. I prayed over it. I talked by e-mail to the missionary from Scotland who was looking for someone to come and teach music in their Bible school there. It didn't feel right, so I abandoned the idea.

The 1993 burgundy Lumina that I bought with the proceeds from selling my house lasted eight and a half years, but by 2001 it had seen better days. One of the men from the church in Buna told me about a home-health care company that sold its used cars.

I bought a 1997 Toyota Corolla with no frills for $7,000. It did have a tape deck, but the windows were hand-powered! At least it was newer, had fewer miles on it, and was less likely to break down during my many travels. After I finished paying for the Corolla, I began to save money for a better and newer car! I had a green Toyota Camry in my mind, but God is famous for His exceeding abundance!

Vance, Dana, and the kids came to visit me on Memorial Day weekend, and Vance told me about a '98 Lexus he had seen for sale next door to his church. He called the owner and found out he was asking $11,500 for the car but had accepted an offer of $10,250. Unfortunately for the seller, but fortunately for me, the person had not returned with the money. The owner of the car was willing to sell it at the $10,250 price.

I didn't have that much money saved, of course, but with my savings, the money I earned from selling the Corolla, and a loan from the credit union I became the owner of a 1998 Lexus GS 300 with plenty of frills! Can you guess what color it was? GREEN!

In November 2001, I had an opportunity to go to Mississippi with Grant and Kellie. He was going for a quick meeting with Brother Mallory and Brother Carney. On our last night there, Brother Mallory unexpectedly spoke to me in the Holy Ghost. He said, "Keep on doing your music well. Keep on the path. God has your life planned. He has your husband taken care of. It has been a lonely road, but you have fought a good fight." Oh, for the Lord to say you have fought a good fight! (Thankful tears!) And yes, I realize that there is still no husband in my life!

In 2002, I was asked to help plan and teach at the Texas Music Festival, a district-sponsored music conference. It would take place the first three days of camp meeting and involved a special singing on Monday night. It was great to be involved in music in the Texas District.

Before that happened, on a Wednesday night in April, I prayed awhile before going to bed, asking the Lord for something more. I loved the Sylvesters and the Buna church, but I wasn't completely satisfied just doing the music there.

I woke up around 2 a.m. I had heard music. It sounded like a cross between wind chimes and a music box. I got up and went down the hall to the living room where a lamp was burning. I heard the music once more, and then there was silence. I thought I had heard the wind blowing the wind chimes on the carport, but no, there was no wind. I went back to bed.

By the next morning, I had forgotten all about hearing the music in the middle of the night—until lunchtime. I was eating with my sister Nelle—whom we called Puge—when I remembered the music.

"Puge," I said, "something strange happened last night." I told her about the music, and she said, "God is gonna give you another song!"

A couple of weeks later at Ladies Conference, I was walking by a pastor's wife I had known for a long time. She called out, "Billye, Billye, Billye, where are you going?"

I said, "I'm going to meet my friend."

"No, *where* are you going?" she asked again, with emphasis.

I told her about the music I heard.

"It was a messenger!" she said.

"But I didn't get a message!" I exclaimed.

She told me that I had just begun to receive the message, and that the Lord would reveal His plan step-by-step.

At that same conference, I thought I heard the Lord speaking to me that I would go to a Spanish-speaking country. I must have been right because later I went to Panama and Puerto Rico on mission trips with Texas Bible College.

By the end of April, I had heard the news that Texas Bible College, a.k.a. TBC, was moving to Lufkin and that the new president was looking for music faculty—a Dean of Music, and a part-time instructor. I sent him my resume, believing that this was one of the steps God was directing me to take.

I was hired part-time, and my friend David Geri became the Dean of Music. I continued serving as the music director in Buna and commuted weekly to Lufkin to teach seven hours of music, plus piano lessons. At that time, we had no senior music majors—just freshmen and juniors—so I would only need to teach on Tuesdays and Wednesdays and could go home on Wednesday afternoon. It would pay the huge sum of $25 per hour taught.

David Geri, Gill Larsen, and me.

CHAPTER FOURTEEN

A New Song

On September 3, 2002, Brooke Elizabeth Bowman was born to Vance and Dana. She had some breathing problems and spent some time in the NICU, but she recovered. We were thankful for another girl and grandchild number five!

In August of 2002, Texas Bible College opened its new campus in Lufkin, Texas, after being in Houston for thirty-seven years. We had fifty-four students that first year. Brother James Boatman was the President.

I drove to Lufkin from Buna every Monday. For two nights, I slept in a room in the girls' dorm, then I went back home to be the music director in Buna.

When I left Jackson, I didn't think I would ever go back to Bible college work, but I was wrong. I taught at TBC for 23 years before retiring! God was certainly directing my steps when I put in my application to teach.

The first few years at TBC were definitely a building and transition process. The college had a Music Department on the Houston campus, but very few curriculum materials had survived the move to Lufkin.

Brother Geri and I started from scratch with the know-how we had gained from being students and instructors at JCM. We had two upperclassmen and about ten freshmen. Somehow, we survived that first year, and so did our students!

By the time school was out in May, I knew I would be hired as a full-time instructor in the fall. I had already talked to my pastor, and he had received a call from TBC's president. My next year would look very different.

Since TBC was a three-year Bible college at that time, Brother Geri and I would have to teach all three years of music classes. It came to a grand total of twenty-six hours of music instruction, which meant thirteen hours for each instructor, plus keyboard and organ lessons.

Brother Geri also directed the choir and chorale. I directed two smaller groups, a ladies sextet, and the men's quartet. We also served on weekend crusades at various churches as time permitted. My duties as music director continued in Buna on most weekends.

Remember the wind chimes I heard and my sister's feeling that I would write another song? During my first semester at TBC, I taught a music composition class. We studied different styles of gospel music and each week the students were required to write a song. I had no idea I would end up writing one as well!

One Sunday morning during the Sunday school lesson, Brother Sylvester said something that did not seem to fit with his lesson's topic. He said, "We need to hold fast to the things that we know are right!" Almost immediately, a little chorus started going through my head.

Hold fast to Him who hath called us. Hold fast to what we believe. Hold fast; don't ever give up. Jesus is coming! Hold fast.

I wrote the words on the Sunday school leaflet I received from the ushers that morning. The next time my class met, I sang the chorus for my students. They quickly picked it up, and we sang it together. One of my students, Lori Green—who is a songwriter herself—suggested an ending. On the last day of class, we recorded the song for me to keep.

During the spring semester, when the faculty and students met for early morning prayer, I began to ask the Lord to give me verses to the song. Months went by and no inspiration came.

On a weekend crusade during the following fall semester, we attended church on Friday night and outreach on Saturday morning. I ran home that afternoon and laid down to rest while a load of laundry did its thing. I was so tired! Then, suddenly, words and a melody came!

The world is getting darker. We struggle through the night . . . We dare not walk by sight. Looking unto Jesus, the author of our faith, we will make the journey by His amazing grace!

I had to get up from my nap to write! God's timing is definitely not ours, but I have found that when we stretch ourselves beyond what we think we can do, God steps in and makes a way.

By Monday morning, I had all the words except the third line of the first verse. On my drive to Lufkin, I was listening to a book on tape when I heard the words, "There are many dangers." That was it! The verse was complete.

The world is getting darker. We struggle through the night. There are many dangers; we dare not walk by sight. Looking unto Jesus, the author of our faith, we will make the journey by His amazing grace!

I sang the song at my church and at my son's church. I shared it with my students, the Dean of Music, and my family members.

A couple of years later, I was at a gospel singing and heard the group Greater Vision. A friend of mine had pitched my song, "God Works the Night Shift" to Rodney Griffin, a member of the group and a prolific songwriter, so I had a reference point to approach him. He asked me if I had written any more songs and so I told him about "Hold Fast." He asked me to send it to him and gave me his card. Wow!

A few weeks later, Bethany was with me when my phone rang. It was Rodney. He told me he liked the song and felt it would bless people. He wanted to put it under contract for two years to see if he could get it recorded for me.

What an honor! As it turned out, he was not successful, but just knowing he thought it was a good song has blessed my life.

Me, with the first TBC Quartet at the Lufkin campus.

CHAPTER FIFTEEN

Chorale Tour

One of my regrets about my time at JCM was not being in the Chorale or going on the summer tour with them. It sounded like so much fun, but I chose not to participate because I thought I would stick out like a sore thumb due to my age and gray hair!

God has a way of turning everything around, even our inferiorities! As a music teacher at TBC, I have been on MANY chorale tours. They are both exhausting and exhilarating!

In June of 2004, we went on a very interesting tour. The air conditioner went out on the bus, but the tour continued. We went to churches in Louisiana, Alabama, and Florida. It was so hot, and everybody was grumpy! We were all getting on each other's nerves. Two girls even got in a fistfight, and one received a black eye! Brother Geri had to call a special prayer meeting to calm everyone down. Thankfully, we did have a great service that night!

During the rest of the trip, we sang at a homeless shelter and at the Windsong Ranch in Arkansas which ministered to drug addicts. We went to Tupelo Children's Mansion and sang and interacted with the kids there.

We had just arrived back in Texas on the last night of the tour when our bus broke down. We waited at a closed service station until after midnight for another bus to come and get us. What fun times!

Every year's chorale tour is different, but each is full of adventure, great memories, and awesome moves of God's Spirit.

The trip from 2016 really stands out in my mind. The summer tour included stops in Marshall, Texas; Little Rock, Arkansas; Duncan, Oklahoma; Wichita, Kansas; Colorado Springs, Loveland, and Denver, Colorado; Tulsa, Oklahoma; and Hurst, Texas!

In Duncan, Oklahoma, the students worked hard and helped to remodel the church. They ripped out carpet, put in landscaping, helped organize the storage areas, and worked on the sound system, among other things.

That night after the church service, an unusual thing happened. After eating, the students began to filter back into the church and a dynamic prayer meeting broke out that lasted for two to three hours. So many things were accomplished in the Spirit that night. It was like the Lord was honoring their sacrifice for helping at the church earlier.

Of course, there are always things going on with the students during a tour. We always had the boyfriend-girlfriend dynamic and drama. Sometimes a couple is breaking up; sometimes they are getting together. Some students experienced things they had never done before. For example, there was one girl who had never ridden in a taxi until we went to Chicago on tour. One girl did a face-plant off the platform at a church in Dallas. There is usually one day that we schedule some fun and visit an amusement park.

Being a part of the chorale is a great way to develop young people for ministry. Brother Horsley, who later came to serve as the Dean of Music, once said that when he first came to Texas Bible College, he could hardly get the students to go and pray for people during the altar services on chorale tour. As the years have gone by, now he can hardly keep them on the platform because they are so eager to go and pray for others.

The TBC Choral outside of the bus on one of our tours.

CHAPTER SIXTEEN

Another Move

The year 2005 started with a bang! As if I didn't have enough to do between TBC and Buna, I decided to take a Spanish class at Angelina College, the community college in Lufkin. The Geris encouraged me in my endeavor and even paid for my book and workbook. I had wondered if I could make it in a secular college setting, and I found that not only could I survive, but I could thrive! I took all four semesters of Spanish classes they offered and kept a 4.0.

In April, the college board ratified Reverend Bret Cooley as the new president of Texas Bible College. We were so excited! Our friends the Cooleys were moving to Lufkin! Our enrollment numbers took a big jump that year.

That year, I also moved to Lufkin, lock, stock, and barrel! I've always wanted to use that saying! The Sylvesters retired from pastoring in Buna, and

I resigned as music director. I no longer made the weekly, sometimes twice weekly, trek to Buna. I also moved out of the dormitory and into an apartment.

More changes at TBC included the addition of Reverend Ron Wofford as the Dean of Theology. He was one of my instructors at JCM. Reverend Cai Larsen also joined the staff as the Dean of Christian Education. It felt like a JCM reunion to me! Some people even jokingly called TBC "JCM West!" TBC was blessed to obtain these quality instructors.

2005 was an eventful year! Hurricane Katrina hit New Orleans and the Mississippi coast, and Hurricane Rita hit Texas and Louisiana. We had evacuees, police, and National Guardsmen on our campus for weeks.

My ex-mother-in-law passed away in 2005 as well. We had been pretty close at one time, but the divorce and distance had separated us. There was no ill-will between us, just neglect of the relationship.

Since I was no longer working for a church, my weekends were free as long as the college did not need me. Occasionally, I had the opportunity to visit a church as a substitute keyboardist; it provided some extra income and I could be a blessing at the same time.

The best part about my free weekends was that I was able to travel to see my kids and grandkids more often. Grant was pastoring in Kentucky, so I usually traveled there only once or twice a year. Vance and his family were in Oklahoma, and I was able to go there over a long weekend or on a holiday trip. Bethany and her husband Chad were only forty-five minutes away in Jacksonville, Texas. They probably got a little tired of seeing me!

In the spring of 2006, TBC held its first Higher Ground Music Conference. The conference was one of Brother Geri's dreams. He planned the conference after the pattern of Jackson's NMMC. Brother Geri named the conference and was the driving force behind it. We all pitched in to help: Sister Cooley, Sister Larsen, our music office secretary Jennifer Cornejo, and myself. We wore ourselves out with many late nights and long hours at the music office, but it was worth it! We had 163 attendees at our first conference.

During the conference, I unfortunately developed shingles as a result of all the work and stress. I was fine during the weeks leading up to the conference, but on Thursday during a class I was teaching my left side started to hurt and the pain continued throughout the night and the next day.

On Saturday I traveled to Oklahoma, and when I arrived, I showed Vance and Dana a sore that had developed on my skin. There was only one sore, but they suggested I go to a walk-in clinic.

The doctor there happened to be from Texas. She said it was a classic case of shingles and prescribed some medicine for me. Some people break out in multiple sores. I only had one sore, but I had plenty of pain! Since then, I have tried to pace myself a little better. It took nearly eight weeks to get over my sickness.

CHAPTER SEVENTEEN

Triumph & Tragedy

In November of 2006, Faith Tabernacle in Arlington, Texas, dedicated their new church building to the Lord. Two of my sisters and I were able to be there for the services.

Brother T. L. Craft, the former President of JCM, was the evening speaker. On Saturday night during his message, he stopped in front of me, took my hand, and said, "I believe someone walked this property praying over it and claiming it for God years ago."

"My mother did that!" I replied. Brother Craft led me to where my sisters were sitting. He wanted to know who walked with Mother. I pointed at Nelle and said, "Her son."

Sometime between 1963 and 1966, Mother had taken her grandson Jerry and marched around the property three times for three Sundays in a row. The church did not own the land at that time, but now, years later, a beautiful church sits in that very location! God never forgets! Even though none of our family lives in Arlington now, I'm so glad we were able to be there that day to celebrate with the church family.

In March of 2007, our second Higher Ground music conference was a great success. Over 300 people enrolled. Then in June, tragedy struck TBC when our beloved Dean of Christian Education Reverend Cai Larsen died after an accident as he was cutting down a tree in his backyard. He was only 34 years old and left behind a wife and three young children. He had a huge impact on our students during the two short years he was with us.

On December 29, 2007, Miranda Suzanne Roberts was born in Oklahoma while Bethany and Chad were there to help Vance at the church. She was a cutie with lots of dark hair and chubby cheeks.

The year 2008 brought two unexpected changes that impacted both my life and Texas Bible College. Brother David Geri resigned as the Dean of Music and Brother Scott Popec was hired to replace him. My son-in-law, Chad Roberts, was brought on board as the Promotions and Alumni Association Director.

These changes were a mixed blessing to me. Brother Geri and I worked together at JCM and TBC. We were and are still close friends. The Geris had been my family in Lufkin. God was moving them away, but He had brought my "real" family a little closer at the same time.

There has never been a loss in my life that God did not send a gain, something or someone, of equal or greater value. I have found this concept to be true over and over again. Brother Popec and I developed a great friendship and working relationship, and it was a joy to have my family close by.

That year, my grandsons Zach and Zathan Bowman won first place at the National Junior Bible Quizzing Championship Competition in Branson, Missouri. We were all so proud of them. So much work goes into a quiz team. Parents and coaches spend a lot of time and effort to make each tournament a success. My son and his wife were the kids' coaches, and they did a great job!

In March 2009, the TBC Missions Club took a week-long trip to Panama. The Dean of Missions

Brother Gary Carter, asked if I would like to come along as a chaperone. Would I? It would be a dream come true. It would only cost me $600.

My daughter helped me make a flyer which I sent out to family and friends to raise support, and it wasn't long until more than enough money came in to pay for the trip and to purchase a nice camera to record the memories.

It was a busy trip as our group landed in Panama. After arrival, we immediately went to a conference in Santiago. We stayed at the Hotel David.

We sang, preached, did outreach, and prayed at the altar. After that conference, we went back to Panama City, where we worked at a home missions church, painting, grouting the floor, and replacing the ceiling. We also bought ceiling fans to be installed after we left.

Then we did more preaching and singing. We also had a fun day when we visited the Panama Canal and took a—very fast—boat ride on the Chagres River which is part of the canal. What a blessing it was for me to be a part of that trip!

Going to Panama was my first official mission trip, but it wasn't my last. A couple of years later,

I was privileged to go to Trinidad, and the year after that I went to Puerto Rico. I think the most impacting thing about mission trips is not the outreach or the services where people's lives are changed, but meeting loving and hospitable saints of God.

Our group went to help the churches in Panama and Trinidad, which were the poorest countries we visited, and in return, we received gifts from them. Even though they didn't have nearly as much materially as most Americans have, they loved to share what they had with us, whether that was a meal or a small token of appreciation.

In San Juan, Puerto Rico.

CHAPTER EIGHTEEN

Growth

There is never a dull moment around a Bible college. In May 2010, Brother Popec resigned from being the Dean of Music, and Brother Timothy Hall came on board. His wife also came to the school to be the Dean of Christian Education. What an addition they were! She had 14 years of experience as a public-school educator, and he had both taught in public school and had been the music director at various churches.

Brother Hall's skills on the keyboard and in vocal performance brought the TBC Music Department up several more levels. There were two live recordings during his tenure.

TBC broke its Lufkin attendance record in the fall of 2010, with a student body of 127! I think my son-in-law had something to do with that . . . Of course, I know there were many factors that contributed to the increase in registration, but I stand by my opinion!

Evan Bryce Roberts was born on August 12, 2010, around 11:25 p.m. He had lots of black hair and weighed eight pounds thirteen ounces. He was grandchild number seven!

General Conference was in Houston that year, and we had record-breaking attendance there also. Sister Gill Larsen and I shared a room, and I had a wonderful time with family and friends. All of the services were so good, and we had a great turnout at the TBC reunion after the Friday night service.

One of the most memorable experiences of the conference was running into an old friend from TBC who attended the same year that I attended, 1964-65. It was an odd thing that I ran into him at all. Gill had gone shopping that day and was late getting back to the hotel, so she told me to go to church without her.

I had quite a time finding a place to park but finally found a lot that ran on the honor system. As I was walking up to the box to pay for parking, I heard a young man telling his friend that he didn't have change, so he was going to have to put in $20.

I checked my wallet and had two $5s, one $10, and two $20s. I laughed and told the young man, "If I give you change for your $20, I will have to put in $20!"

And then I thought, I will just give him $5. He didn't want to take the money, but I said, "Just put some money in the offering!"

An older couple was walking away, and the lady said something about the cooler weather and her husband asked me where I was from. When I said I worked at TBC, he said, "I attended there in 1964 and 1965." That's when I stopped to take a good look at him. I didn't recognize him, so I asked his name.

"Larry Neal," he said.

Oh my, what a surprise! We had run with the same circle of friends. What a blessing it was to see him again. He is quite a good musician and had recorded a piano solo album which he sent me a few weeks later.

Enclosed were copies of two letters I had written to him years before. Enclosed also was a copy of a card I had sent him with only three words, "I am praying." He had kept those things at least forty-three years!

I don't remember sending the card, but he said he had been going through a severe and lengthy trial when he received it from me and that it had meant so much. I think it is impossible to know just how much we have impacted others' lives as we live ours. Oh, the blessings God sends our way. So many that are unexpected, but just what we need at the time.

CHAPTER NINETEEN

Traveling, Words, & Performances

In March of 2011, I went with the TBC group to Trinidad on a mission trip. Brother and Sister Landaw were the missionaries there and in Puerto Rico. We had four church services and one street service. We reached out to the community and painted a church.

On the trip, I met a lady named Lynn Lamont. Her husband was the superintendent of the work under Brother Landaw. She and I made a special connection and occasionally still keep in touch with each other thanks to social media.

Back in Texas, I went to play the keyboard on several Sundays at Brother Pound's church in Beaumont when Sister Pound was out. On one particular Sunday in 2011, Sister Toni Holst came up to me after the service to give me a word from the Lord.

She told me, first of all, that the Lord had heard my cry. Secondly, that He was working some things out on my behalf. Third, there was a change coming. She said the change was something big that would mark my life and that when it happened, I should let her know about it wherever she is. She said when it happens I would look back and recall our conversation. Oh, thank You, Jesus! You are good to give us encouragement along our way!

In 2011, we were in the middle of a drought and everything on campus seemed dusty, but the rain of the Spirit was on the way. Our enrollment for the fall semester that year was 141! We just kept growing!

On the 20th of September 2011, we had some distinguished guests visit our campus. Our special guests included Aaron Lindsey, the producer for Israel Houghton and Marvin Sapp, Daniel Johnson of New Breed, and Terence Jones. They came to hear our chorale sing and to talk with Dean of Music Timothy Hall about producing a live album for TBC. They were very nice and down-to-earth.

Aaron Lindsey ended up producing the recording in January of 2012. It was the first recording that TBC had made in quite a number of years.

Our Legacy Youth Conference continued to grow, and in January of 2012, there were so many attendees that we had to turn people away from the Friday night service. The Lord continued to bless our conference over the years until it was discontinued.

One day, at a senior fellowship at Cornerstone UPC, my friend Irene Oliver spoke to our group. At the end of her talk, she used the scripture II Corinthians 4:7, "But we have this treasure in earthen vessels, that the excellency of the power may be of God, and not of us."

What was strange about her using that verse was that Vance and I had just talked about the exact passage of scripture a few days before, and he had used it in a class at TBC on Monday. He also heard Brother Russo, our district superintendent, use it at a funeral the same day. About a month later, I was talking to a young evangelist who quoted the same verses.

When these repetitive things happen to me, I know the Lord is trying to tell me something. Nothing with God is a coincidence. Halley's Bible Handbook, explains the passage as describing the sufferings of Paul and that with all he had gone through, he must have come to the conclusion that he was invincible until the Lord was ready to call him home! Oh, to always have that confidence!

February of 2012 brought the Texas District Singles Conference that happens here in Lufkin every year. Brother Jeff Story gave me a word from the Lord during the conference. I especially loved the last part of what he said to me. "Jesus wants you to know that you've had faith in Him, and He's had faith in you, Sis!" I started my new journal with that story.

In April 2012, I was able to travel to Puerto Rico for another mission trip. I loved the way the saints sing and rejoice even after the formal church service is over. They were very musical and demonstrative in their worship. One of the keyboard players played strictly by ear because he was blind. The pastor, who had rheumatoid arthritis, played the bass for the song service. It's so good to get out of our little world and see that there are people all over the world who love God like we do! On a little side note, our group saw Rick Santorum, who ran for the Republican nomination for President of the USA in 2012, and his wife, marching in a parade in San Juan!

On Friday, April 13, 2012, my sister-in-law Bessie passed away. With help from Bethany and Dana, I provided the music for her funeral. I still miss her. I was only 17 when she married my brother, and she always treated me like her little sister. We had very few "moments" over the years when we disagreed, and I knew she loved me unconditionally.

Over the years, I have had the privilege to play the music, or at least help with the music, for some of the funerals of some of the older saints from my church in Arlington: Sister Naomi Campbell, Brother and Sister B.C. Cain, and Sister Charlene Toerck, to name a few. These were some of my favorite people, and I miss them all.

In November of 2012, the students at Texas Bible College presented "The Gospel According to Scrooge" for the first time. It was a live musical performance directed by our own Timothy Hall. The first year was awesome and it was even better the next year. The performance was as professionally done as many shows I've seen at Branson and at other entertainment venues. It was a great experience; every performance revealed the hidden talents of our students.

The TBC group in Trinidad.

The TBC group plus a few extras in Panama.

CHAPTER TWENTY

New Things

In January of 2013, I bought my second Lexus! It was a 2006 model, which brought me up a few years. It was the first time in my life I had paid cash for a car! Actually, many years ago, my husband and I did pay cash for a car, but this purchase was all on my own. Thank you, Dave Ramsey, for your wisdom.

On January 22, 2013, my son-in-law Chad Roberts was voted in as the pastor in Marshall, Texas. My daughter was expecting their third child during that time, and Chad was still working at TBC, so for several weeks he and I rode to Marshall together for church. He was preaching and I was responsible for the music.

On February 11, Colin Wade Roberts was born. He weighed in at eight pounds and fourteen ounces. He was born with a small amount of blond hair. After a few weeks of recovery and adjustment,

Bethany was able to take over the music at the church. They were still living in Lufkin, but once the semester was almost over, they moved into the parsonage connected to the church.

I spent a lot of the summer of 2013 going to Vidor to play the keyboard for the church there. I would drive over on Saturday and stay with my sister Shirley. I would play on Sunday and stay through the Wednesday evening service. I would drive home to Lufkin on Thursday only to repeat the cycle on Saturday again. They paid me well, and I grew to love and appreciate the Edwards family, along with several other church families there.

In September, my sister Puge turned 80. Her family threw her a big party. Her entire living family was there: her four children, their spouses, and all the grandchildren and great-grandchildren.

Later that month, my friends the Huckabys celebrated their 40th anniversary, so I traveled to DFW to be there for them. I gave a little speech telling everyone how much the Huckabys have meant to me.

The Huckabys moved to Arlington from Pine Bluff, Arkansas, in the 1980s. Mike came first to look for a job and a place to live, and then went home to get Sharon and their three girls. When they walked in on a Sunday morning, I knew I wanted to be Sharon's friend.

Our kids were close to the same age, and we spent a lot of time together. We gave each other nicknames. She is Obie Jean, and I am Sybil. When my marriage fell apart, she was one of the first people I called. Without hesitation, she said, "Send the kids over here." When I moved to Jackson, she helped me pack even though she was not happy about my leaving her.

Sharon came to my graduation, and we have stayed friends over the years. Sometimes my kids and I had Christmas at the Huckabys' house, even though they might be gone for the holiday. If we came to DFW for anything, we could stay at the "Huckaby Hotel."

When I had surgery, Sharon came to Lufkin to help me. And when I retired and was moving, she came to help me pack again! I am thankful we now live close to each other again! Everyone needs a friend like Sharon (and Mike) Huckaby.

With my friends, Mike and Sharon "Obie Jean" Huckaby.

In January of 2014, my grandson Kendall turned 16. Grant and Kellie gave him a special party with a knighting ceremony that was very touching, welcoming him to adulthood. In May, his sister Kaylie graduated from high school. Watching them grow up made their Grammy feel like she was getting old!

In February of 2014, TBC's second live recording directed by Tim Hall was completed at The Anchor Church in Beaumont. The album is titled "In Jesus' Name" and is a great representation of Texas Bible College and Holy Ghost-anointed singing by dedicated young people. They also included some older alumni in a couple of songs.

In March, the chorale went on our Spring Tour. I found out that Brother and Sister Hall would be leaving at the end of the semester, but the students weren't told until a month later. There was "weeping, wailing, and gnashing of teeth" at that announcement.

In May, I went on my first cruise with the TBC Senior class of 2014. I enjoyed it a lot. It was a weekend cruise, and we only made one stop in Cozumel, Mexico. What fun times! The singer in the rotunda was especially good. He could sing song after song without any music in front of him. I made great memories!

On July 14, 2014, I received a text from Brother Cooley letting me know he had resigned as president of Texas Bible College. In a specially-called staff meeting the next day, we found out that Brother Carl McLaughlin would be the interim president for an unknown period of time. When Sarah asked about the Dean of Music, Brother McLaughlin said he would call Brother Hall and ask him to stay. He agreed to stay one more year, thank You, Jesus!

In August, the TBC staff enjoyed a retreat at the church in Euless where Brother McLaughlin pastors. Everything was great and we had a good time. One of the most interesting things that happened while Brother McLaughlin was president was the institution of online classes. We had talked about offering online classes for years, but it was finally coming to pass.

On Vance's birthday, August 22, during our "Happy Birthday" call, I happened to mention that I wanted to go to Israel. The thought had been building up inside me for a while and suddenly became a burning desire. I had never really wanted to go before. In September, my first paycheck reflected double the raise that Brother Cooley had given me four years before. I now had the money to go to Israel but no one to go with.

I went to Mineola for my brother's birthday and told my niece Darla about my desire to travel to Israel. Her friend, Gena Caruthers, just happened to be going to Israel along with her husband David, and a group from their church. She gave me Gena's phone number and that's how I took my first trip to Israel.

We left on December 27, 2014, and were gone for ten days. I can't even put into words how much I love that place! As we were traveling from Galilee to Jerusalem on the bus, we could see the lights of Jerusalem up ahead. They played the song "Jerusalem" through the speakers on the bus, and, well, my emotions spilled over and drained down my cheeks!

At the Sea of Galilee, one of the girls said, "I know it's just water, but I love this!" I felt the same way. I tried to participate in everything. I rode a camel, waded in the Dead Sea, and climbed the En Gedi mountain!

I met a Jewish schoolgirl at Caesarea and took a picture with her. She wanted to know why we were visiting Israel, and I said that we love the Bible, and therefore we love Israel. She asked if I was a Christian, and I said, "Yes, are you?"

She laughed and said, "Oh, no! I am Jewish!"

What a tremendous blessing the Lord bestowed upon me to let me experience all of that.

Me on the tour bus in Israel, 2014.

My first trip to Israel with a group from San Antonio, 2014-15.

CHAPTER TWENTY-ONE

Happy Birthday!

My oldest sister Betty passed away in March of 2015. Siblings are very hard to lose, and she was my first sister to pass away. We have all tried to stay pretty close as a family, so this was a difficult time for all of us. Thank God for preachers in the family, and also for singers and musicians. I guess that is something that we have taken for granted. It is such a blessing!

Bethany and Chad's two oldest kids, Miranda and Evan started Bible Quizzing in 2015. Miranda was seven years old, and Evan was only four, but they did remarkably well and placed fifth at the Spring Extravaganza! If you want to see and hear something cute, have a four-year-old quote verses from Proverbs!

In April, we found out that Brother Gary Carter had been selected to become the new president of Texas Bible College. Brother McLaughlin had only been the interim president, and we needed a full-time, on-site leader.

On May 11, 2015, I turned 70-years-old. My kids threw me a surprise birthday party at Cornerstone United Pentecostal Church. So many friends and family gathered to honor me. All of my kids and grandkids, plus my brother, long-time friends, fairly new friends, and somewhere-in-the-middle friends were all there. It was wonderful! Both the Princes and Russos came to the party. It is pretty great when a District Superintendent and former District Superintendent attend your birthday party! My life has been tremendously blessed! I'm so thankful!

On May 22, my friend Sarah Johnston, a TBC alumnus and fellow teacher, married Cody Ashworth in Starks, Louisiana. Sarah graduated in 2009, and, after being away for a year, came back to TBC to teach and work in the front office. She had lived in the "Guidroz cabin" on campus during the school year and in the dorms during the camp season. After she was gone, my daughter suggested that I ask about moving into the cabin myself.

I hadn't really considered it before, but I moved in after getting permission from the district. The cabin was built sometime in the 1950s because that is when the campground officially opened. It belonged to Brother V. A. Guidroz, the district superintendent during the 1950s and 1960s. I lived there for nearly ten years. It only took me a couple of minutes to get to my office and classrooms—a tremendous hardship!

Not only did we get a new president in 2015, but Brother Hall officially left in May. Brother Dwayne Horsley was hired as the Dean of Music. Along with him came his very talented wife, Diane, their son Ian, and their dog, Mika.

Brother Horsley graduated from JCM in 1991 and is the same age as my older son Vance. I had met him in 1997 at a music conference in Jackson and I had not seen him since then. I knew from different reports over the years—mostly from David Geri—that Brother Dwayne and Sister Diane would be great assets at TBC. The years since have proven that to be true.

TBC made two live recordings during their tenure, which are both splendid albums. Our Music Department grew and was a lively and welcoming place for students to learn. We graduated some knowledgeable young people who are helping prosper the kingdom of God.

The North American Youth Congress for the United Pentecostal Church was in Oklahoma City in 2015. I still wish I had gone even though I was in the process of moving and having trouble with my knee from all the walking I did on my trip to Israel. I would have loved to see nearly 25,000 young people in one place at one time, all praising the Lord. I believe they broke some kind of sound barrier!

Brother Lee Stoneking said that when we let our voices out in praise, we "sheer the air." The Bible says the devil is the prince of the power of the air, so let's praise the Lord loudly, cut through the air, and change the atmosphere!

In the family, my ninth, and last, grandchild was born on December 10, 2015. Mason Hugh Roberts weighed in at nine pounds, six ounces, and twenty-one inches long! He looked quite a bit like his mother's baby pictures!

In 2016, my oldest granddaughter, Kaylie, married Frankie Maruzzi, and Zach graduated from high school. Chad's mother, Sue Roberts, who had conspired with me to bring our children together, was set free and refilled with the Holy Ghost that year.

My sister Shirley and I traveled to New York City with our niece and her family. We had such a great time. It was another of those trips that happened because I mentioned to someone that I wanted to go. About three months later, the Lord opened the door for me.

My son-in-law was busy with the church in Marshall. Not only was he preaching, but he was also leading the service and teaching the adult Sunday School lesson each week. I offered to teach the adult lesson, and a few months later, he took me up on it.

I taught for the first time in June of 2016. After that, I taught about once a month. It was one of my greatest joys! I loved studying and putting the lessons together.

In 2016, TBC reinstituted our Higher Ground Music Conference with great success. We had about eighty attendees.

Shirley and me at the Empire State Building.

My home for the last 10 years. The Guidroz cabin on the UPC Campground.
Bro Guidroz was the Texas District Superintendent in years past.

My 70th Birthday, with all my family; including my brother, Charles.

CHAPTER TWENTY-TWO

I Will Live & Declare the Works of God

I have always wanted to go to California and drive the Pacific Coast along Highway 1. In the summer of 2017, as a graduation present for Kendall, Grant and Kellie decided to take him on a trip. They went to Palo Duro and the Grand Canyon, then on to Las Vegas. They asked me if I wanted to join them there. Of course, I did!

They picked me up at the airport and we drove through part of the Sierra Nevada Mountains to Bishop, California, where we spent the night. The next day we visited Yosemite National Park. It was absolutely beautiful! Then we went on to San Francisco.

We stayed close to Fisherman's Wharf, rode a trolley downtown, drove down the most crooked street in America, and across the Golden Gate Bridge through Sausalito. We hit Highway 1 to start up the coast and drove all the way to Seattle. I saw some of the most beautiful scenery that I've ever seen.

I came home from that vacation just in time to attend the viewing and funeral of my good friend, Sister Irene Oliver. She had passed away while I was gone. She was 97 years old, and I had known her since I was very young when we all lived at Silsbee.

I spent quite a bit of time with her in the last few years of her life, since we both lived in Lufkin. She always used to tell me, "Now you can only do one thing at a time, so concentrate on what you are doing until you finish that and then go on to the next thing!" She had a remarkable memory and sometimes she would sing me a song or quote a poem for me. Now I wish I had recorded her.

In August of 2017, Hurricane Harvey, a category four hurricane, hit the coasts of Texas and Louisiana, causing terrible flooding and quite a few deaths. The TBC students, along with our president and his wife, went to Southeast Texas to help some of the saints of the churches distribute food, water, cleaning products, and paper goods. Some of the students worked to help clean out debris from damaged houses to make them ready for reconstruction.

That same month, my friends, the Halls, celebrated their 50th wedding anniversary at the church in Arlington. I was privileged to attend the party, especially since I was the maid of honor at their wedding all those years ago!

During the course of the event, I talked to Pastor John Harris for a little while. We talked about how old we were becoming, and he shared a scripture with me.

He said, "You're going to live a long time."

Then he wrote Psalm 118:17 down on a piece of notepaper, "I shall not die but live and declare the works of the Lord." I had that handwritten note on my fridge for years. I love the promises of the Lord, and I had a lot of confidence in Pastor Harris.

In January of 2018, I was chosen to teach the "Keys to Success" class at TBC. We had lost a Bible teacher that semester and I offered to teach as a replacement. Brother Carter assigned this class to me instead. It was a challenge.

I had to keep the attention of forty-eight rowdy freshmen and try to teach something that would help them navigate their lives with "success." It was the only time I have taught a non-music class at the college, but it was a good experience for me. I hope it was for the students too!

In May of 2018, we graduated our largest senior class that we had at the Lufkin campus. Twenty-six graduates received their diplomas. The Texas District Board and the Texas Bible College Board voted for TBC to pursue accreditation. They hired Dr. Ralph Buie to come aboard to help with the transition.

TBC has been in the process of seeking accreditation for several years now. Most of the instructors are working on or have completed their master's degrees. I did not try to do that because Brother Buie told me that because of my age and teaching experience, I could be grandfathered in and continue to teach until I retired!

Also in May, my grandson, Zathan, graduated from high school and received a basketball scholarship for a college in Oklahoma. He had already signed the paperwork to start in the fall and decided at the last minute to attend church youth camp that June. At camp, the Lord began to deal with him about preaching the Gospel. After a series of confirmations, Zathan became my first grandchild to attend Texas Bible College. He has now graduated.

In September, I attended my 55th high school reunion. In October, Grant and Kellie celebrated their 25th wedding anniversary. In November, they became grandparents when their daughter Kaylie gave birth to a beautiful baby girl, Eloise Grace.

That same day of joy was also a sad one. My friend Pat McInnis, who had run the cafeteria at TBC for thirteen years, passed away from the effects of a stroke.

In December of 2018, my grandson Zac was a student at The University of Oklahoma (OU). He was just about to take his finals for that semester when he had a couple of fender benders within eighteen hours of each other. He hit his head both times. He ended up experiencing retrograde amnesia. When Vance and Dana arrived at the hospital, he did not know who they were.

As the days passed, he regained some memory, but could not recall the last nine or ten years. He could not remember any of his high school years, or what classes he was taking at OU. He did not remember that he was a mascot on the spirit team, or that just the week before he had been at the Big 12 Championship Game.

Zac has always had a great memory and was a national Bible quizzing first-place winner when he was 12 years old. When he finally went back to the doctor, he didn't receive a lot of encouragement. The doctor said he believed Zac's memory would return a little bit at a time over the next year few years but that it would be sporadic, and he would have to fit the pieces together like a puzzle. The next five months were pretty difficult for the Bowman family, especially for Zac and his mom and dad.

On vacation with Grant, Kellie, and Kendall in 2017.

On vacation with Grant, Kellie, and Kendall in 2017.

CHAPTER TWENTY-THREE

Precious Miracles

In May of 2019, the TBC chorale was scheduled to sing at the church in Shawnee, Oklahoma where Vance pastors. I was traveling with them. I had not gone on the chorale trip the previous year because I felt I was getting a little old. I changed my mind and was determined to go again. Besides, this time they were going all the way to California, and I wanted to be there.

It was Monday, May 6, when we arrived in Shawnee. The service was power-packed with the presence of the Lord from the beginning. When the chorale started to sing "Your Blood," the soloist, Hunter Mahaney, said he felt a healing spirit in the room. As the students began to sing, the Holy Ghost was moving, and some of the students left the platform to pray for different people in the audience.

I did not see what was happening because I was on the other side of the building, but three of the guys began to pray for my grandson, Zac. I was sitting on a little altar bench when Andrew Summit came over, sat down beside me and said, "Sister Bowman, your grandson remembers everything!"

"What?" I asked. I was not thinking about Zac's memory being healed. I stood up and made my way over to where Vance, Zac, and Brooke were embracing. The Lord had restored his memory immediately and perfectly! No bits and pieces to put together; it was all there in a moment's time by the mighty hand of God!

As we traveled further west on the tour bus, I was able to share Zac's story with some of the churches where the chorale sang. It really seemed to encourage and uplift the saints of God and we had some powerful services the rest of the trip. Even our bus driver received a special healing at one of the churches where we sang.

That summer, Zac decided he would not return to OU but would come to TBC to fulfill God's call on his life. He has since graduated from Texas Bible College.

In March of 2019, I went on another trip to Israel with a group from Vicksburg, Mississippi. The group included my former pastor and his wife, Brother Don Tipton and Sister Tipton, and my good friends, Heather and Mark Hughes.

Israel was just as great the second time around, and I would probably go again if given the opportunity. It is my favorite place on this earth! Of course, I haven't been everywhere!

My second trip to Israel with a group from Vicksburg, at the Garden Tomb.

My sister Nelle, or Puge as we call her, turned 86 on September 17, 2019. Her children planned another get-together for her, but they didn't plan on Tropical Storm Imelda. Puge lived in Vidor, and there was extreme flooding there and in the surrounding areas. A couple of family members were stranded and could not travel, so the party was canceled. I decided to go anyway just to visit her, and I'm so very glad I did.

We talked a lot. Well, mostly I listened while she reminisced of things that happened a long time ago. I went home on Monday, and Puge had a stroke on Wednesday and fell and broke her foot. By the end of the week, she was placed in a nursing home near where her daughter lived. While there, she had a slight heart attack, went to the hospital, and then was put on hospice care.

I made a couple of trips to Glen Rose, Texas, to see her before she passed away on November 19. One of the hardest things I have done was to sing and play at her funeral, but I did it with help from my daughter, daughter-in-law, and niece. Puge is buried by our Daddy in the McKinney Cemetery north of Kountze, Texas. I miss her terribly.

She was the nearest thing I had to a mother since Mother died when I was 29 years old. I can't even begin to put into words how I leaned on her over the years. She was always there, and my biggest fan. She was also the family historian and had researched much of our family's genealogy. She is irreplaceable!

In March of 2020, the COVID-19 Pandemic became prevalent in the world. After two weeks on spring break, Texas Bible College students left campus, and classes went completely online to finish out the semester.

I had never taken an online class in my life, and suddenly I had to learn how to put classes online for my students. With a lot of help from Brother and Sister Horsley, I made it through and completed the task at hand.

On May 11, 2020, I turned 75 years old! I could hardly believe it myself!

In June, I tested positive for COVID-19 and was sick for several weeks. I was exposed at church. We had about twenty-five cases in all at the church. My case was not severe, but it was long-lasting.

Finally, after five weeks I retested and received a negative result. It took a couple of more weeks before I felt like myself again. It is a very weird virus. I lost my taste and smell and ran a low-grade temperature for days. Since so many people younger than me have died from this virus, including too many of our precious ministers and saints, I can only thank the Lord for my life and determine more than ever to live it pleasing to Him.

In December 2020, I was involved in a terrible car accident. My sister Shirley was with me in the car, and the other vehicle was a motorcycle carrying two people. Both the driver and his passenger were killed.

I don't know that I have ever been as devastated as I was that night. Knowing I had caused someone's death just sent me into a dark hole I didn't think I could climb out of. The accident was on a Saturday evening and on Monday morning, Brother John Boone called and prayed for me. I will never forget some of his words.

On Tuesday night, my brother called and prayed for me. He had something similar happen to him and understood what I was feeling. After those two prayers and many others that were prayed, I began to climb out of the hole. I still wish that it hadn't happened at all, but God has helped me to be able to function daily without being emotionally crippled by what happened. My insurance company took great care of me and paid me well for my car. They also settled the death claims without adding any more liability to me.

In February of 2021, we had a "snowpocalypse" here in Texas. On campus, we had to cancel classes as we were without water for three days! Thank the Lord the electricity was mostly on for the duration of that time. Very interestingly, the students really enjoyed the snow! I enjoyed seeing the pictures. Most years, we did not get snow there.

My brother Charles passed away in March of 2022 and left a huge hole in my life. He was a spiritual counselor. My sister Shirley passed away in 2025 on June 26 after nearly 11 years of fighting cancer. She put up such a valiant fight. She was not a loud person, but she was a strong one. I miss her so! She was such a giver - what a blessing she was to me.

It is strange when you no longer have siblings, especially when you're the baby of the family and your siblings have been there your entire life. I still haven't quite figured out how to navigate life without them.

My children and grandchildren are doing well. Vance and Dana still pastor in Shawnee, Oklahoma, and have recently purchased a larger property that they have remodeled and dedicated to the Lord. From two acres and a small building to six acres and 12,000 square feet—what a transition! All three of their children are pursuing ministry.

Grant and Kellie live in Crowley, Texas, south Fort Worth, and own two florist shops that are doing well. Their two children have made them grandparents five times.

In January 2024, my son Grant was valet parking at a hotel in downtown Fort Worth when a gas leak caused an explosion, and he was seriously injured. We don't know how far the accident threw him, but he has had multiple symptoms, including PTSD and PBA, hearing loss and tremors, and balance problems. We are trusting that the Lord will heal him in His time. I am so thankful that the Lord spared his life.

Chad and Bethany's kids are thriving. They are smart and talented. God has been so good to me! Chad was elected Secretary of the Texas District United Pentecostal Church in September 2021. Not long after, he and Bethany moved to Lufkin to live, and I was very happy about that!

Texas Bible College is now under the leadership of Dr. Eugene Wilson, as Brother Gary Carter left at the end of the school year in 2021. TBC is still pursuing accreditation. Even though enrollment is somewhat down, the spirit and quality of students is still excellent.

I decided to retire in May of 2025, as I turned 80 years old on May 11. How did I grow this old while I was not paying attention?

Since the United Pentecostal Church only has a few Bible colleges, and only so many positions available at each one, I was very blessed to be a part of that ministry and to have a place to work for the Lord.

Most people retire around the age of 65. When I was about 65, I began to think—and talk, and pray—about retirement. I never felt it was time for me to retire. As the years rocked on, I felt I still was contributing to TBC in an important way.

In March of 2024, I attended the dedication of my son's church in Shawnee. At the end of the service Brother Ricky Garza gave me a word from the Lord. He said, "You don't need to worry about money for retirement. God will supply the money for the things you want." It was odd because on the way to the service, I had said to my son-in-law and daughter, "I just want to take the money I've saved for retirement and travel."

In late May, I was visiting Grant and Kellie when Brother Horsley called me and told me he had resigned as the head of the Music Department. When I told them the news, Kellie immediately said, "Well, Mom, you can just move in here with us. You'll have a private bedroom and bathroom. You can come and go as you please, and it won't cost you anything." Grant agreed with her.

I began to pray about turning in my resignation before the fall semester started, but after talking to my pastor, his advice was to wait, so I did. I think

I enjoyed teaching more than ever during my last year at TBC.

In March of 2025, in a chapel service, Brother Wilson prayed for me and told me almost word for word what Brother Garza said. He added, "What you have given to TBC, God is going to give back to you." It was the confirmation I was listening for. I knew it was time, and I talked to Brother Wilson about retiring shortly after that day.

It was a difficult decision. I loved my job and teaching young people. I knew my income would be greatly affected, but I had God's promises. I decided I would move in with Grant and Kellie.

TBC honored me at a chapel service and gifted me new luggage, a quilt signed by students and faculty, and a engraved plaque thanking me for my 23 years of service to the college.

In the meantime, Chad resigned as District Secretary and began to evangelize while waiting for direction on a pastorate. In April 2025, he was elected to pastor in Midlothian, Texas. It is a growing town in the Dallas-Fort Worth metroplex, not far from Crowley where I live with Grant and Kellie. Now, I am commuting to church, teaching the youth class, and helping with music. We're all excited about what the Lord is doing here.

I know I have come full circle. I lived 30 years of my life here in the Dallas area, and after pursuing God's will in Mississippi and East Texas, I am back home and loving it.

It's difficult to know how to write the ending of a book when God is still doing so many wonderful things in my life. As I look back over every blessing and every challenge, I can see God's hand guiding me. Every day is a precious gift and miracle. I will spend the rest of my days declaring the wonderful works of God!

Me, with Bethany's family.

Me with Grant's family.

Me with Vance's family.

My entire family at my 80th birthday and retirement party.

Epilogue

This is a story I have enjoyed sharing over the years, sometimes with my students, and sometimes with my family and friends.

In 1987, I was learning to walk by faith. At the time, I was working at Texas Drug Warehouse, a deep-discount drugstore. The store had a special area where they kept close-out items—merchandise purchased from stores that were going out of business.

One day, we received a close-out shipment of Dr. Scholl's sandals, and they were marked at only $5 a pair. Those shoes regularly sold for about $30.

I wanted a navy pair, but I let several days go by before deciding to buy them. For me, $5 was hard to come by. When I finally went to purchase them, there were no navy shoes left in my size, only burgundy.

I was disappointed but decided to buy them anyway. I took the shoes to the service desk, wrote my name on the box, and asked them to hold them for me until the next payday, when I could purchase them.

A week or so went by, and when I finally paid for the shoes and opened the box, they were navy! Navy! How did they change colors?

I don't know the answer to that, but I DO know it increased my faith. I learned that God is watching out for us, even in the smallest details of our lives.

During the four-year ordeal before the divorce was granted, I had so many expressions of encouragement from my sisters and brothers in my church family. One Wednesday night after church, Sister Pat Dudley handed me a little card. I didn't really look at it and just slipped it in my coat pocket. A few weeks later, I was going to have to have surgery, so I had to watch a film in preparation. (This was before the days of Internet!)

After the film, I stopped to get some lunch. I was apprehensive and feeling anxious about everything. When I reached in my pocket to pay for my lunch, I found the little card. Here is what I read.

LET GO AND LET GOD

As children bring their broken toys,
With tears for us to mend,
I brought my broken dreams to God,
Because He is my friend.
But then instead of leaving Him,
In peace to work alone,
I hung around and tried to help,
With ways that were my own.
At last, I snatched them back again,
And cried, "How can you be so slow?"
"My child," He said,
"What could I do? You never did let go."

What a lesson for us all to learn. His ways are higher than our ways, His plans are greater than our plans

STAY IN TOUCH

Thank you for allowing me to share my story of God's blessing in my life. He is the one who writes my life song and I find my joy in worshipping Him.

I am honored to have been a part of educating so many wonderful young people throughout the years. I would love to hear from you as I enjoy my retirement.

You can reach me at billyebowman@aol.com.

God bless you all!

Billye Bowman

www.ingramcontent.com/pod-product-compliance
Lightning Source LLC
Chambersburg PA
CBHW050940050726
47592CB00007B/2374